THE FUTURE IS GREATER

by

JOY. C. AGWU

Publications

ISBN: 978-1492719922

Typesetting, page layout and cover design by:
DocumentsandManuscripts.com

Cover illustrations used courtesy of openclipart.org
(lake scene) and Wikimedia Commons (*Aino from the
Kalevala*, created by User Eino81)

All artwork has been reproduced on the
understanding that it is in the public domain. This
assessment is based on the most reliable information
available at the time of going to print.

Published with the assistance of **The Manuscript
Publisher**, publishing solutions for the digital age -
www.TheManuscriptPublisher.com

The Future is Greater

CONTENTS

PART ONE

Is Suicide the Answer?

Victoria and Mary are good friends. They go to the same school and they both live in the same estate in Tralee, County Kerry. Victoria was born in Nigeria but came to Ireland when she was young, in the company of her mother and her other siblings, Christian and Charity, while Mary is Irish.

A few years ago, a fifteen-year-old girl took her own life. It was shocking and very difficult for Victoria and her friend Mary to handle. Even I, as an adult, being Victoria's mother, found it very difficult to comprehend. This incident created worries and a lot of questions among Victoria, her siblings and her peers, including Mary, Victoria's friend.

One bright Saturday morning after breakfast, Victoria and Mary came to me while I was looking through my window, watching the birds of the air twittering and flying around. They asked me a question: 'Why would anybody want to take his or her life?'

So I said to them, "People do take their lives when they think that the world and humans have rejected them; when they feel hopeless and conclude that their situation is irreversible."

I turned and looking at them; I saw the anxiety on their faces. I asked them, "Have I answered your question?" They kept quiet and looked at one another. 'One more question,' they whispered.

"Alright," I said, "let me have the question." They continued whispering. Suddenly Mary said, "No it is fine," but Victoria asked, "What is the most important thing in this world?"

"Life" I answered, "your life is the most important thing in this world because it is very precious and it has no duplicate. You are only you, there is no other you, and as far as your life is concerned, you are the most important person in the world, because you are alive. Therefore, where there is life, there is hope, hope of a better tomorrow and a greater future because greater things are coming ahead. And it is only when you accept yourself, challenge your challenges, forget the failures of yesteryears, yesterday and today and keep pressing forward that you will see and enjoy the beauty of life."

"Mom," Victoria called, "why is it that some people are poor and some people are rich?"

Mary supported saying, "Oh yes! Some people are tall, some are short, some are ugly, and some are beautiful while some people live in big houses and some live in small houses."

So I answered, "All these are just to maintain equilibrium because nobody is better than the other. We all have one life, one life with different destinies. Everybody is unique in his or her own way. Some people are poor," I added, "but I can move from point A to point B yet my bills are not much, but they are paid. The rich man has food on his table and I have food on mine. It might not be delicatessen like that of a rich man; but it is good for my system. The dresses I wear are not expensive but they fit me. You have a boyfriend and you broke up with him because you were not compatible and he is not good enough for you. He found another girl but he can never prevent the next day from coming. There is always another tomorrow which is greater. The rich live in big houses and we live in small houses, but they will only sleep in one room at a time, just like us, and that makes us equal. They have ten wardrobes of different attires and twenty wardrobes of different handbags and shoes but they will always wear one at a time, just like me. For that reason, I have no respect for status. What someone is means nothing to me. They sleep, I sleep; they wake, I wake; they eat and I eat regardless of the condition in which all of these things are done. We are all the same, because we do the same thing every day. And we all have one life."

Having said all this I asked Victoria and Mary whether I had answered their questions. "Yes" they answered. "It is more complicated than we thought," they whispered to one another.

"No there is no complication here," I continued, "I am going to tell you two stories, after which you may use your own judgement. One is about a rich man who loses all he has to the hands of armed robbers. The second one is about a boy whose parents are poor."

"Once there was a man in my village in Anambra state of Nigeria, nicely dressed, who was attacked by armed robbers." I began the first story ...

This man was driving his beautiful jeep and armed robbers took all he had, including his jeep, removed all his expensive clothes leaving him with only underwear. He looked at them and said 'fools, what I have is more important.'

The armed robbers were very angry because he called them fools, despite all they took from him. So they brought him into the car at gunpoint, took him to his house and took all he had, including all his life savings and left him naked, took him back inside the car and drove a far distance, where he was unable to locate his home and pushed him by the roadside after beating him. They looked at him to see his reaction, only for him to call them fools once again. At that point, they did not know what to do with him anymore, so they left him and fled.

This man lost all he laboured for over the years in one day, but when he managed to stand up, he said 'thank Heavens, the one thing I have is more important than the ones they took, at least I am alive. But they already know that today or tomorrow may be their last day. Tomorrow I am going to have a new beginning. The future is greater.' He reassured himself and went in search of help.

After the story, I called the two girls and asked them what they learnt from it; they answered simultaneously, "No condition is permanent, things can change over time."

"Yes! That is exactly it; no condition is permanent," I repeated and continued, "because change is constant. That it is going well today does not mean that it will go well tomorrow. Someone might be laughing this minute; the next minute tears might be flowing like a river from his eyes. Everything happens, both good and bad, in order to maintain balance. If you fall today, it is because you are going to rise tomorrow; you cannot leave your back and front doors open at the same time because you cannot be in two places at the same time. There is always time for everything, time to plant and time to harvest; time to be born and time to die; time to rise and time to fall; time for sorrow and time for joy. If the world is just full of happiness and no sorrow, then we would have had a universe of stupidity and lunacy."

Mary and Victoria started laughing. Then I said to them, "Oh! You can laugh; but did you remember when Kerry played football against Dublin and Dublin won?"

"Yes! Yes!" Victoria and Mary shouted. "We were so sad that we were unable to eat, because we hoped that Kerry was going to win as usual."

Then I said to them, "Kerry did not win because the Sam Maguire cup was not destined for them. They went there with the hope to win and Dublin went there hoping to win also. It was the time for Kerry to weep while Dublin laughs, because the almighty Kerry have been smiling and laughing for years. But because of human selfish desire, Victoria in particular," I said and pointed to Victoria, "told me that the referee was against Kerry."

"Mom is very mean to Kerry," Victoria whispered to Mary.

Although I heard their whispers, I pretended not to have heard; but when they stood up to go, I asked them a question, "Is suicide the answer?"

They were surprised, so they kept quiet, whispering, 'If we say yes she is going to ask another question, and if we say no she may still ask a question, so let's say we don't know.' After a while, they said they did not know.

Then I said to them, "I know the answer so can you sit down?"

They sat down and also came Christian, Charity, Sandra (who is Charity's younger sister) and Molly, Sandra's friend. I asked all of them to sit down, that I was going to tell them a story of a teenage boy from Africa who wanted to take his life.

So I began the story with the introduction: "He is an only child who feels lonesome at home, his name is Ogeechee. This boy is never happy because his parents are poor. Holidays are his worst days especially long holidays."

PART TWO

Looking for what is not Lost

Ogeechee's parents were very poor and Ogeechee was an only child. He was always sad because his parents are poor. He cried sorrowfully behind closed doors, unknown to his mother or father. This had been happening from the time he was a toddler to this day, when he is now a teenager. One Saturday morning he stood up and went to the mountain, looking up to the clouds to see if he could get an answer to one of the numerous questions that went through his mind; he did not get the answer.

So he asked himself, 'Where do I get the answers from? I do not want to talk to any human beings because they are no help. Human help does not last,' he continued to ponder.

He looked up to the clouds again and said, 'Maybe I should ask this cloud, who knows he might have an answer at least to one of my questions. You never know he might, and if he does answer one, well what can I say? Ah ha that is a starting point.'

He asked the cloud, "Why am I born to suffer?"

He waited for a very long time, but the cloud never spoke to him. Then he left the mountain and went to the valley. He sat down and started talking to himself.

A lot of noise was coming from every direction, as it was the time of day when people go to the stream to fetch water, but he did not hear anything, because he had gone to the great beyond. Even hunters were going hunting with their hunting dogs, running and barking, yet he had no idea of what was happening around him. As he was sitting there, gazing into the speechless cloud, he fell asleep. When he woke up, he discovered that his hunting bag was gone.

He said to himself, 'I wanted to set a trap to see if it could catch an animal, so that my parents and I could use it for supper tonight. I wasted time looking for what is not lost.' He continued, 'what have I achieved? What am I going to do now?' He found himself in a fix: to go home or to set the traps?

As he stood blaming himself an unknown old man came to him with an alternative suggestion. He said, "Take your life but before you do it, please give me your shoes so that I will have a feel of shoes on my feet, because I have never worn shoes before."

He looked at himself and kept quiet.

Then he lifted up his eyes and said to the man, "Why do you want my shoes? And why are you telling me to take my life?"

"Oh! You want to know?" the man asked.

The teenage Ogeechee said, "Oh yes I want to know."

"Okay, every day you come here and stand, gazing into the empty air, looking for what is not lost. Simply give me those shoes and go to the other side of the planet; there you will meet the ones who never talk. In case you do not understand me," the strange man continued, "you should join your ancestors so that your worries will be over, and when you get there, just tell them I said hello, that I will join them when my time comes."

"Oh!" Ogeechee screamed, "So your time has not come and you are older than I am? I am asking you, respond, you crafty cruel old man."

"I am not just older than you are: I am old enough to be your grandfather. Ah ha, you said I am crafty and cruel. What of you? Have you not been very cruel to yourself? I asked you a question too; respond, you selfish greedy pig," the old man shouted.

"Okay, I now know," said Ogeechee. "So because you want my shoes those are the reasons why you advised me to take my life; is that it?" he asked.

"Yes that is the reason, but that is not all. Before you take your life, please take me to your house, so that I will inherit all you have, including your parents if you have them, because I do not have any. Come with me," the man continued.

Ogeechee followed him and he pointed to a cave saying, "This is where I live, there are lots of ropes here, look at that one there," the old man pointed to one. "It is very strong. I can give you that one and if you want. I will help you to tie it on a tree so that you can easily hang yourself with it," the old man advised.

The angry Ogeechee was confused, so he looked at the old man and asked, "Are you mad?"

"Oh! Exactly the second question I wanted to ask you. You are a mad and selfish boy, if not I do not know the reason why you come here every day to disturb me. See the rope, take your life; let me have your inheritance. After all, I have nothing to lose, but you have parents, do you not? I do not know if you do, but if you do, they will be the ones that lose, not you. If I inherit them, at least I will have a house and stop living inside this cave. Please decide what you want to do fast; let me know where I stand," the old man beckoned.

"I can see that you are the devil itself. Let me leave here now so that you can wait for your next victim," Ogeechee said as he was about to leave.

"Oh I forgot to tell you," the old man shouted, "one more thing please."

"And what could that be?" Ogeechee asked.

"I took your bag while you were snoozing away over there," the old man confessed.

"Why did you take my bag?" Ogeechee asked.

"Because you do not need it. I had already seen that you were on a suicide mission: that was why I came to help you. But you do not want to see reason with me. Please do it fast; let me decide what to do with my inheritance," the old man urged.

"So, because I have a problem, and I came here to relax and think, the only advice you could give me is to take my life so that you can take my inheritance? Yet you have not even thought of what you are going to inherit: whether it is a perpetual poverty. And you want to inherit my parents also," Ogeechee continued.

"You see, we are still saying the same thing, and even you are worried about what I am going to inherit," the old man maintained. "That one has nothing to do with you; just do what I asked you to do. Leave me to handle that one; when I get to that bridge I will cross it," the old man explained.

The angry Ogeechee hissed and said, "Give me my bag let me go home."

"Oh, wait a minute, so you have a home? Have you parents as well?" the old man demanded to know.

"Yes I have parents. What else do you want to know?" Ogeechee asked.

"Everything: so that if you do what I am telling you to do, it will be easier for me when I come into your family. I will not have much to explain to your parents; I will just take over so that they will not grieve so much. Come to think of it," the old man continued, "you said you have been coming here to think, but your thoughts could not help you, so how long are you going to continue thinking?"

Ogeechee became very angry so he said, "Give me my bag, you strange aberration of nature in the form of an old man."

"Come closer. Come and take. I do not even need it. Stay there. Wait for me," the old man said and went inside the cave. The next minute he came out with a very sharp knife.

At the sight of the knife, the anxious Ogeechee ran away and the old man started chasing after him saying, "Go and thank your stars. Next time, if I see you here, I will cut you into pieces, since you can be this selfish. You are tired of life and I am not. Instead of you helping me, by doing what I told you, you stood here asking for your bag. I made a mistake: I should have taken those shoes from you a long time ago. Fool! You are running for your life, yet you pretend to be tired of life. If I ever see you around here again, I will help you to end it fast. Come back here again, one more time, if you ever see the daylight again; know that my name is no longer Zumba but idiot. You have a home," he continued, "which is not enough for you. I live in a cave and you came here to disturb my little life. If you miss your steps again and come into this forest,

I will show you the quicker way to your ancestors," the old man said and went into his cave. Taking the hunting bag he stole from Ogeechee, he started dancing and singing.

PART THREE

Perseverance is the Key

The next day, Ogeechee woke up in the middle of the night, pondering over what the old man told him. His mother went to his room and asked him why he was not sleeping. He said he had a dream and woke up, but could not go back to sleep. His mother requested to hear the dream; he refused, so his mother went back to bed.

Later that morning Ogeechee stood by his window gazing into the empty horizon. He went out again, this time to the beach. As he was sitting by the roadside, he became bored and decided to go on to the beach. When he remembered what the old man told him, he said to himself, 'This is the moment of truth, thank God and thanks to that old man in the cave for saving me from my foolish decision that would have destroyed the happiness of my parents and my friends. Enough of this self-defeat. After all, I am young, things will get better when I grow up; yes things will get better' he repeated. So he was happy once again.

As he removed his clothes and prepared to jump into the water, he did not know that a mad man was hiding in the bush, watching and listening to him. When he turned his back to jump into the water, the mad man jumped out, took his clothes and his shoes, and ran away. Ogeechee chased after him

The mad man was wearing only underpants and Ogeechee was wearing only underpants; passers-by were looking at the two of them. When Ogeechee saw that the mad man was running faster than he was, he cried out for help. The passers-by started running away, crying out for help, shouting that two mad men were trying to attack them.

Ogeechee felt humiliated and went back to the beach. There he saw a group of six to eight years old children playing. At the sight of him, the children ran away whispering to one another that Ogeechee was the mad man they saw few minutes ago. Ogeechee became very angry and felt disgraced; so he went home and quickly changed, as his parents were not at home.

Later in the afternoon, he went back to the beach and saw the mad man wearing the clothes he took from him. Ogeechee was shocked, so he asked him, "You again? What are you doing here?"

The mad man ran away saying that he had seen a mad man.

"Stop there!" Ogeechee said, "I have a question for you."

The mad man stopped and said, "Alright, quickly, let me have your question."

"Why are you wearing my clothes?" he asked.

"Oh your clothes! I thought you would have been dead by now. What are you waiting for?" the mad man asked.

"I thought you are insane?" Ogeechee asked.

"And I thought you are mad?" the man responded. "I had been watching you while I was hiding in the bush. You were talking alone. I checked everywhere and did not see a second person. So I felt you did not need the clothes, and since I do not have any, I was very happy. At least for once, I am dressed well. Moreover, this is my territory. Anyway let me advise you," the pretend mad man said, "if we continue to think about our predicaments in life, we may take a wrong decision. Come with me, young man," the old man requested.

Ogeechee was reluctant, so the man said "No, come with me, nothing is wrong with me: I was only pretending to be mad. I just want to show you something."

The old man took Ogeechee far away into the forest and brought him to where he lives under a tree, in a hut built with bamboo. He asked him to sit down and Ogeechee sat down. Then the old man said to him, "Look around you and tell me what you see?"

"I can see some trees, leaves, bushes and some flying birds," Ogeechee responded.

"Is this place not quiet and peaceful enough?" the old man asked.

"Yes it is," Ogeechee responded.

"The world is beautiful, and life is very sweet." Ogeechee was very surprised to hear a lonely old man who lives in the forest confess that the world is beautiful and that life is sweet. Ogeechee was quiet for a while, so the old man asked him whether he was all right. Ogeechee managed to say yes.

The old man took Ogeechee farther down into the forest and showed him desolate and shattered old buildings. Then they went back up to the old man's house, where Ogeechee took his time and looked around and observed that the forest is full of old and shattered houses. He was puzzled but then he managed to say, "Oh heavens! These are old houses." Ogeechee continued, "Where are the inhabitants of these lands? What happened to them? Where did they go? And why did the jungle return?"

"It is a long story," the pretend mad man responded. "You do not want to hear it, do you?"

"Oh yes I do," Ogeechee responded eagerly.

"It is not what you want to hear, young man, do not destroy your ears. So go home and have your dinner, stay with your parents and come back another day, because it is getting dark and your parents will be worried."

Ogeechee insisted that the old man must tell him the story but the old man bluntly refused. So Ogeechee asked him to take him home, as he was afraid. The old man followed him. When they got close to his house the old man told Ogeechee to run into the house while he watched. Ogeechee looked back and said, "My name is Ogeechee, what is your name?"

"My name is Eric," the man answered. They shook hands. Ogeechee pleaded with Eric to come into his house and meet his parents, but Eric refused. So Ogeechee ran into the house and Eric went back to the forest.

Ogeechee's mother stood in front of the house worried and anxiously waiting for him. His father, in the meantime, had gone to the neighbours and his friends in search of him. Ogeechee apologised for coming home late but when his father came back, he restricted him from going to the forest to see Eric. Instead, he was made to go stay with his grandparents, who lived in the next village. Ogeechee, who was very happy with his newfound friend, was disappointed at this. Moreover, it was during the long holidays. Although Ogeechee liked playing with his friends, he preferred going to the forest to stay with Eric. Eric, for his part, was missing Ogeechee.

One afternoon, Ogeechee was eating his lunch with his parents when he heard a sound like that of a cricket. He quickly recollected that Eric used animal sounds to call him, as Eric knows how to make all kinds of animal sounds. So he ran out to meet Eric. Ogeechee sat down under a mango tree with Eric and Eric started telling him stories as usual. Ogeechee's parents waited a long time but he did not come back to finish his food. So Ogeechee's father went in search of him, only to find him sitting under a tree right in front of their house with Eric. Ogeechee's father was surprised when he saw his son with a strange old man right in front of his house. Ogeechee stood up as soon as he saw his father saying, "Dad, my friend Eric that I was talking about," pointing to Eric.

Ogeechee's father asked Ogeechee to go and finish his food, while he talked to Eric. Following their discussion, Ogeechee's father found Eric to be very interesting, so he then permitted Ogeechee to visit Eric. However, he insisted that he must go early, as it is a very long walk to where Eric lives. Fifteen-years-old Ogeechee was very happy, so the next day, after breakfast, the happy Ogeechee went to see Eric. When he got there, he made an animal sound, just as Eric does. Eric quickly ran out to meet him. As soon as Ogeechee saw Eric he shouted, "The story, Eric, the story."

Eric laughed and asked Ogeechee to sit down. Ogeechee sat down and said, "Yes I asked some questions the other day, but in case you have forgotten: Where are the inhabitants of this land? What happened to them? Where did they go and why did the jungle return?"

"Many years ago," Eric began his story; "there was a tribal war in this village of Ngwuba. Back then, it was the tradition that any tribe that wins the battle has authority over the other. The other tribe becomes their slaves. This village was unfortunate, so when the battle ended the other tribe took all the young women and children, leaving the old people behind. The young men and women that managed to escape were scattered everywhere. The majority of them migrated to the city and many died, leaving their parents heart broken. My parents died during the tribal war. I was twenty-six years old then.

After many years of wandering in the wilderness, I returned to this village. When I came back, this place was desolate. I stayed many days without food or water. It was only the kindness of the animals that kept me alive. This place was inhabited by gorillas, monkeys, baboons, all kinds of animals. It was one old gorilla who gave me fruits and taught me how to survive in the jungle. The animals are very friendly. I learnt a lot from them and they learnt a lot from me. I thought it was the end of my life but the animals gave me a new hope."

"Where are the animals?" Ogeechee asked. "I have not seen any animal around here," he explained.

"They have gone to a faraway land," Eric explained. "When it is evening they will return."

Ogeechee maintained that he was going to stay until evening to see the animals, despite all the pleadings by Eric. So when it was evening Eric brought out an animal horn and blew it so loud that many animals gathered around. All the animals were very angry when they saw Ogeechee; they saw him as an intruder. They were so angry that they wanted to attack him. Then Eric made a sound and one gorilla clapped his hands and all the animals lined up in a single file. When Eric blew the horn again, the gorilla clapped; all the animals sat down in a circle and Eric and Ogeechee sat in the middle. Eric brought his flute and started making lovely tunes and the whole place was as silent as a graveyard. After about an hour one monkey went in to Eric's hut, brought out a drum and started beating it, while Eric kept blowing the flute. At the end, the animals departed to their hiding places.

Ogeechee was amazed with what he saw, so he yelled out to Eric three times saying, "Unbelievable! What is happening here?"

"Fragments of a wild civilization," Eric answered.

Ogeechee still could not comprehend what he saw. He yelled out to Eric, "This is unbelievable, animals playing drums, clapping hands and sharing food like humans; what could this be? Is it a warning to us that are still the inhabitants of this world? Or a window to the past life of the ancient men that lived in the caves?"

"Well done," Eric said and clapped, "you are a very intelligent young man. It is both." Eric continued, "First it is a warning to people like you, who are very young, restless and tired of life; when they have not accomplished their mission in life. You came into this world for a purpose, and that purpose you must find out and fulfil. You have to learn to take each day as it comes. When I thought all hope was lost, these animals gave me hope. Here I am living in the jungle, with happiness in my heart, having lost all the members of my family, my friends and relatives. Today I have a new life. If I am happy, living with animals, you should be happy living with your parents. Time: it is only time that heals the wound. All it requires is patience, contentment and diligence. Whatever you are going through in this world, definitely somebody somewhere is going through the same thing, or even something worse than yours.

"Perseverance is the key. So never try anything stupid, because it is not the solution. It is only the coward who runs away from challenges. No responsible human being runs away from responsibility. It is our responsibility to stand upright and mastermind our destiny by being optimistic. Your destiny is in your hands. Your parents are poor so that you can stay positive, think big and become rich.

"Secondly, young man," Eric continued, "it is indeed a window to the ancient lives. In those days, ancient men lived with nothing; but they enjoyed life with little or no resources. They lived like birds of the air. They were satisfied with what they had and they lived longer; unlike today when death is becoming a game that men play, both young and old, because of greed and selfishness.

"The ancient men ate good foods, drank water from its natural source and they were satisfied. There were no orthodox doctors and medical practitioners; they believed in the ancient traditional way of treating illness and it worked for them, because they had faith. In the world of today, we have big names and incomprehensible medical terminologies for diseases; and the diseases are getting unimaginably smarter than we can handle, because we are over-exaggerating and creating fertile grounds for them.

"We are living in a universally totalitarian world. We develop technologies that we cannot control. It is not going to get any better; it is going to get darker and suicide is not the answer. The answer lies there with you, and what is that? You might want to know.

"The answer is resilience; you have to learn how to take each day as it comes. In the midst of every problem lies the solution.

"Young man," Eric called, "it is getting dark, I must take you home now but you must listen to this:

'We want to fly like birds
Yet we have no wings.
We want to build castles in the air
Yet we have no wisdom.
We want to fast-forward the hand of the clock
Is that not self-deceit?
And then you ask, why?
Because you cannot delay
Or fast-forward the work of nature.
Yet the clock is man-made.
We question our existence
Yet we have destinies to fulfil.
We want to live today and die tomorrow
Because of selfish desire.

'We want to acquire all the wealth in the world.
How much did we bring with us

On the day of our birth?
We want to end our lives
To be free from the ups and downs of life
And yet, we left some questions unanswered:
Are we self-made?
Does life really have an end?

"Oh! He took his life.
His days of agony and sorrow are over.
How can you be sure?
What if it is the beginning of another life, in a different
*   dimension?*
I do not have answers to these questions,
As well as you do not have answers to them too.
Do we have rights over our lives?
That I do not know,
But I do know that
The body is just for function
The brain is for intellect and wisdom, but spirits don't
*   die."*

When Ogeechee had listened to Eric's recitation, he was very quiet and very disappointed with himself. Eric noticed it and said to him, "No young man! Do not blame yourself; everything happens for a reason. You have to learn how to turn a negative situation into a positive one, instead of making a stupid decision. It is only a coward that runs away from the reality of life; and you might want to know what I mean by the reality of life.

"What I call the realities of life are the challenges of life. Therefore, stop looking for what is not lost. Stand upright, face your challenges by forgetting the pains of yesteryears and keep pressing forward; because you are going to a greater height, and you are going to use your past experiences to help those who are in similar circumstances, in the near future.

"The future is greater and children like you are the future of tomorrow. We cannot afford to have cowards as the future of tomorrow. These grey hairs may carry enough wisdom but my bones are weak; that is the reason why it is important for me to transfer that wisdom to you. Because my blood is cold and yours is hot, that is why you are young. Hot blood flows through your veins and arteries; that I call the blood of the youth.

"You remind me of the days of my youth. When that hot blood of youth comes pressing the wrong buttons in us we tend to do many irrational things. That is why I always think that children are young, foolish and innocent. So, young man, it is important that we combine wisdom and strength together, because one cannot exist without another. Then you may ask why again. Because the strength of your hand alone cannot give you prosperity. But the combination of the strength of your head, which is wisdom, and the strength of your hands will give you not just prosperity but also longevity.

"Young man," Eric addressed Ogeechee, "I do not mean to confuse you but these are the things that you must know. Write them on your forehead; write them also on the tablets of your heart. Treat them like everlasting treasures, and pass them on from generation to generation. You can start with your friends and relatives and together you can change the entire universe. Did you hear me young man?" Eric asked.

"Yes I heard you," Ogeechee responded

"Very well then," Eric said. "Therefore, stand up and go home and start planning your mission; because you must accomplish it. Maybe when I am gone, because my days on Earth are numbered, as you can see, but you must carry out everything I have said today. Give me an answer," Eric demanded.

"I will carry out all your instructions," Ogeechee replied.

"In that case I have to take you home," said Eric.

"One more question!" screamed the curious Ogeechee.

"Seek to know no more, only remember that the future is in your hands."

When Ogeechee was about to leave, Eric yelled "Ogeechee! I almost forgot; please take these because I do not need them." Eric stretched his hand giving Ogeechee the clothes he took from him. "I took them just to get your attention."

Ogeechee refused and insisted that Eric should keep them, that he needed them more than he did, but Eric laughed saying, "I have no need for it. I am content with what I have. Take them," Eric insisted. So Ogeechee collected his clothes from Eric and went home.

When Ogeechee got home, he was so cold that his parents were wondering what was wrong with him. When they asked him, he said to them, "I learnt a different thing today: what you have never taught me."

Ogeechee's father said to him, "Definitely you cannot learn everything from your parents. There are some things you cannot learn from your parents, which you can only learn from your friends, teachers or from an adult. Only when you seek to know them, and only when occasions call for them. No parents," Ogeechee's father continued, "own a particular child. Children are gifts and those gifts are universal. Therefore, every parent is every child's mother or father; because what I do not have, another father can give you. Only understand that human beings are inter-reliant, both young and old."

"Ah ha," said Ogeechee, "this is another lesson of its kind."

"Yes indeed, a lesson of its kind," Ogeechee's mother supported. "There are things you cannot get from the *Reader's Digest* or the internet." Ogeechee's mother continued, "That is why listening and communication is extremely important. If you listen more and communicate more with friends, you will discover that life is very sweet and simple. These things are easy. When friends gather around, instead of discussing things that will waste your time, share your thoughts and ambitions, things that will move you forward. I mean youthful and fresh ideas; ideas that will bear fruit."

"Oh!" Ogeechee shouted, "What a day. I have learnt a lifetime's lesson in one day. Indeed the world is full of good and evil: the good is to encourage us to keep going and the evil is to make us stronger and more enterprising for a better tomorrow. The world is not perfect; human beings are not perfect either. If the world were perfect, there would be no crime, therefore there would be no police and lawyers. But if we can take each day as it comes, like Eric said, then the world will be a very happy place to live in," Ogeechee concluded.

"Yes my son," Ogeechee's father replied, saying, "It takes only the hand of a man to turn a forest into a dwelling place. Only if we learn to be steadfast, then you, the youth can make the world better. So stop chasing shadows, face the reality; you have responsibility here on earth." Ogeechee's father left as two of Ogeechee's friends entered.

"Dad, are you going?" Ogeechee asked.

"Yes," Ogeechee's father responded, "I have to leave you with your mates."

One of Ogeechee's friends is from a very wealthy family, while the other is from a poor family, like Ogeechee. Ogeechee and his friends started their usual discussion. The other poor boy told the boy from a wealthy home that he is better than him and Ogeechee. He turned the question and said to them, "Please let us leave the better-than-you kind of thing and think of better things. You are talking of my parents, and what they have; but I want to see what I can achieve by myself. Therefore, let us discuss what we want to be in future. Because wherever we are today, someone else had been there before. It is left for us to find out how they got to where they are today and draw up our plans."

"That is the truth!" Ogeechee shouted. "If my parents are poor, that does not mean that I am going to be poor. We have to learn how to be optimistic. We need to learn to live with reality, because the world is not perfect. I learnt big and unforgettable lessons when I was looking for darkness in the midst of light, so both of you give me your attention." Ogeechee then recited a poem:

What a world full of surprises!
I was crying that I have no shoes
And I met someone who has no legs.
I was crying that I wear glasses
And I met someone who cannot see.
I was crying that I do not have a good house
And I met someone who has no home.
I was crying that I could not sing
And I met someone who could not speak.
I was crying that my parents are poor
And I met someone who had no parents.
I was crying that I have few friends
And I met someone who was a loner.
I was crying that I have little food
And I met someone who had no food.
I was crying that I have never eaten to my satisfaction
And I met someone who had food but could not eat.

I was aspiring to be rich
But, when I heard what it takes to be rich,
Then I decided to remain poor.
I was crying that I am not beautiful
Until a met a very beautiful girl who has no brain;
Then I concluded that beauty is nothing.
I was crying that I have no husband,
Until I saw a man who turned his wife into a punching
*   bag;*
Then I decided to remain a spinster for the rest of my life.
I have no money to go the doctor
And I cried out to my neighbour,
Then she took me to the doctor.
When the doctor told me the side effect of my prescription
Then I decided to keep the disease that I have.
I was crying that I never went on holiday,

*Until I saw someone who went to borrow money just to
    eat,*
After she came back from holiday.
Then I decided to remain where I am.

I was crying that my country has no oil
But when I saw what is happening in oil countries,
Then I lifted up my hands
And said thank God my country is at peace.
I was crying that I live in the countryside
*But when I heard the gunshots, noise and crimes in the
    town*
Then I began to adore my country home.
I was crying when I saw my classmate on the stage,
Because I had wanted to be a super star,
But when she told me what she does to keep going,
Then I decided to be proud of who I am.
I was crying that I could not see,
That I cannot walk,
That I am wheelchair bound,
But when I heard disturbing and unbearable sounds,
Like that of a rushing wind,
Then I asked what the problem was
And I was told that
There is chaotic disorder all over the world.
Then I concluded that I am safe,
At least I cannot witness any disorder.

When I think of the never-ending toils,
The never-ending confusion,
The never-ending crimes,
*The never-ending greed, selfishness, dissatisfaction, envy,
    strife*
And every evil thing you can think of,

That has polluted the world,
Then I asked myself what is going on:
Has the world gone mad?
Then I said, no the world has not gone mad.

Again, I looked through my window,
And I saw the sun, the moon, the stars and the clouds,
Then I said, "The world is beautiful."
Again, I began to think of the land,
The seas, the forests, the mountains,
The rivers, the oceans, the trees
And even the flowers.
Then I confessed
The beauty of nature.

I opened my window
And I saw a fly and a buzzing bee
Then I looked up to the mighty sky
And I asked:
"How large unto the mighty sky
Do little things appear?"
I took a walk to the seaside
Then I saw flying birds twittering
And sparkling streams chattering
In appreciation of the glory of God
Then I lifted up my eyes and asked:
"Why can't we thank God?"

I have considered all these,
Then I said
Flying birds do twitter
And sparkling streams also chatter
Even the firmaments sometimes make sounds
To appreciate the glory of God

Yet everything in the world is made for human comfort.
Then I came to a conclusion,
That man is the architect of his own problem.

PART FOUR

We have a Destiny to Fulfil

A few years later, Ogeechee finished secondary school and got admission to the University of Lagos to study engineering. He felt so sad, leaving his parents and Eric in the village, because it took a whole day to travel from the village to the city and at the cost of a lot of money too. So Ogeechee was worried, because he was not sure of the possibility of going home very often to see his loved ones.

When Ogeechee got to the city, he felt very strange and intimidated by the other students, who were from the city and used to city life. He had no friends but, being a very intelligent, optimistic and determined young man, he kept pushing forward in spite of the fact that he was being put down and ostracised by other students. Ogeechee kept struggling, but his worst nightmares were weekends, when he had to remain in his room for fear of being bullied.

One Saturday morning, when most of the students were in their rooms sleeping and some were doing their laundries, Ogeechee quietly sneaked out of his room and went in search of a weekend job. Poor Ogeechee's luck shone on him when he entered a very big hotel and met the owner at the entrance who was just going out.

"Good morning, Sir," Ogeechee greeted him. Being a very big hotel, the owner thought Ogeechee was one of his casual staff, so he asked, "Why are you just coming?"

Ogeechee was embarrassed, so he nervously answered, "Sorry Sir, I do not understand you."

"I mean, why are you just coming to work now?" the owner of the hotel repeated.

"Oh I don't work here. This is the first time I have come to this place. I just came to see if there is any vacancy for a cleaner here."

"Oh I am very sorry young man, forgive me if you can." As the owner was about to go out the door, Ogeechee ran after him saying, "Excuse me Sir, can you please get me a job?"

The owner of the hotel stopped and looked at Ogeechee for a little while, surprised by his courage and ambition. So he asked, "Who are you? What brought you here and have we met before?"

"My name is Ogeechee. We have not met before Sir, but I am looking for a job, and I am just wondering whether I can get help from you."

The owner of the hotel was surprised, so he whispered to himself, 'What a courageous and ambitious young man. I must help him.' Having said that, he told Ogeechee to go into the hotel and tell the receptionist to take him to the manager of the hotel. He told Ogeechee to tell them that he does not work there, only that he has a message to deliver.

As Ogeechee turned to go, he looked back and asked the hotel owner, "Who do I tell him that sent me, Sir?"

"Tell him Eric, Eric Morgan."

"Oh God! What a coincidence!" Ogeechee muttered.

"What is it young man?" The owner of the hotel asked.

"Nothing Sir, I was just thinking of other things," Ogeechee answered.

While Ogeechee went to see the manager of the hotel, the hotel owner sat inside his car waiting, as he had told Ogeechee to go to the manager and come back to him. He kept wondering about the simplicity and the innocence of Ogeechee.

As Ogeechee was leaving, he was so downcast that he forgot that Eric, the hotel owner, asked him to give him the feedback from his conversation with the manager. Moreover, Ogeechee did not know that it was the owner whom he had spoken to. So, as he was walking away slowly, Eric the hotel owner came out of his car saying, "Young man I was waiting for you."

"Oh! I am very sorry Sir. It is just that I did not get the job. The manager said that there is no job for me at the moment; that they had contracted the cleaning to a company," Ogeechee explained.

Eric asked Ogeechee to follow him while he went into the hotel. He told Ogeechee to sit down and asked the receptionist to tell someone from the kitchen department to get Ogeechee something to eat, while he went upstairs to meet the manager. When the manager saw Eric, he quickly explained to him that he could not give Ogeechee any job, due to the fact that they had many applications to consider, that Ogeechee is only a student looking for a part-time job.

"So when did it become a crime for a student to look for a part-time job?" Eric asked.

"It is just that most of the applicants are graduates, and Ogeechee is a student, so I felt their applications should be considered first, more so as Ogeechee did not complete any application, he just walked in and said he needs a job," the manager replied.

"So because he did not apply for the job or submit his CV, therefore he cannot be given a job, even though he has submitted his identity to you, showing how humble and desperate he is, as well as the urgency with which he needs the job? The people you are considering employing, do you know their motive?"

The manager looked surprised.

"Please answer my question, do not evade it; when did it become a crime for a student to look for job?" Eric repeated.

"Well Sir, it is not a crime for a student to look for a job, neither did I say it is a crime but I think it is better for him to face his studies. Most importantly, from my own experience of being a student once, I am always sceptical of employing students, because they are unpredictable."

"Thank God you said you were once a student. So you have an idea of what some students, who come from a poor background, go through to keep on with their studies. So do you know him? And did you ask him the reason why he wants the job?" Eric asked.

"Yes I did ask him and he said that it is to support his parents in paying his school fees," the manager answered.

"That is the reason why you urgently have to give him a job," Eric replied.

"What job Sir? I have already taken his name down and promised him that we will contact him any time we have a job for him."

"That is very good, but in case you have not understood what I said, give him a job, or better still, put his name in the payroll and ask him to come here every weekend and watch television and at the end of the month. Just make sure you give him his salary. Choose between the two and let me know before the end of the day."

"Yes Sir, but …" the manager was trying to say something, while Eric shouted, "Do not but! I have spoken," and he left.

The manager gave Ogeechee a job as a waiter and emphasized that he must put up a good conduct, as he once got into trouble for employing some students, years ago, who stole from them and the clients and then went missing. Ogeechee in turn promised to be a good boy.

When Ogeechee saw that the manager had given him fifteen hours he said, "Sir I can work from 6pm to 11pm on Fridays as my lectures end at 4pm every Friday, then 6am to 9pm on Saturdays and Sundays if you let me."

The manager laughed saying, "Very interesting. How are you going to cope with your studies?"

"Do not worry about my studies Sir. I know how to structure my timetable. Only help me as I have explained."

The manager was puzzled by Ogeechee's type of personality. Not only that, he saw the anxiety on his face. So he stood murmuring, "If I say no, I do not know what the boss will say; and if I say yes, I do not know whether it will backfire against me, if this boy turns out to be a radical who is pretending to be a saint." So he turned to Ogeechee saying, "Young man, come back to me by this time tomorrow."

Ogeechee happily left, and the manager phoned the boss and presented Ogeechee's demands to him. Eric, the boss told the manager to grant Ogeechee whatever he requested, and also to make sure that Ogeechee went back to the campus every Sunday with enough food that would last him for the week. So the next day when Ogeechee went back to the hotel, the manager told him that he could start the next weekend based on the hours he requested.

Ogeechee was very happy when he started the job. He was soon making enough money to buy his books, and also saving some money for his parents. His confidence began to increase rapidly. But he was still feeling isolated by the students, even to the point that they made mockery of him whenever he asked a question in the class. Though Ogeechee tended to ask too many questions in the class, they were always intelligent questions.

One Friday afternoon, during their last lecture, all the students were making haste to go, so that they could go to their various hostels and prepare for parties and clubs. Ogeechee meanwhile, was trying to clarify some aspects of the lectures, so that he could understand everything before he went to his work. But when he asked a question, most of the students said that it was a stupid question. Ogeechee kept quiet. There was prolonged murmurings and shouting in the classroom. So the lecturer got angry. He ordered the students to remain quiet saying, "Silence! Silence every one; as far as this lecture hall is concerned, I am in charge for now, so anybody who is tired can go, and to the best of my knowledge and ability there is no such thing as stupid question in the field of learning. Therefore the only stupid question I know is the one you did not ask."

Four years later Ogeechee finished school and got a job in the city. He built a house for Eric. A few years later Eric died. Ogeechee was very heartbroken, but to keep the memory of Eric alive he built an orphanage in the forest and some residential rehabilitation centres for vulnerable children, and named them after Eric. People started moving down to the place to live again. Just like Eric told Ogeechee, that it takes just the hand of a man to turn a forest into a dwelling place.

After listening to Ogeechee's story the children were very quiet and amazed, at the same time they were very happy that Ogeechee achieved his aim. Most importantly, the children confessed that if Ogeechee had taken his life, or gave up going to school because of the bullying by the students, that he would have destroyed his bright future. While the children were smiling and murmuring about Ogeechee's success, I asked them, "Is suicide then the answer?"

Victoria and Mary said, "Suicide is not the answer; because the future is greater and we have a destiny to fulfil, and Ogeechee's story teaches a lot. With courage and determination you can achieve a lot, no matter who is bullying you."

Christian and Charity said, "No, because we do not even know where our spirits will go after death." They laughed and went away.

Sandra and Molly said, "Suicide is not the answer because we have a lot to enjoy in future."

"Yes suicide is not the answer!" the children confessed.

POSTSCRIPT

Tabula Rasa

Children are the future of every nation: mothers and fathers of tomorrow, heroes and leaders of tomorrow. At the same time, they are the most vulnerable members of the society. Therefore, it is the duty of the parents, teachers, guardians, community and society at large to prevent the children from being harmed, or doing harm to themselves. Provide them with shelter, food and all the necessary things they need as children. Protect them from danger and avoid exposing them to dangers.

It is also good to give them the opportunity to participate in some decision-making, because not only is that freedom a human right; but sometimes they may have the best ideas that can change the whole world. But they have to be given the freedom of speech to express their opinion and they have to be listened to, because children are very sensitive. They have to be handled with care. They love to see that they are valued as an individual and as part of a group.

Children between birth and puberty are already human beings, although they are childish and immature. Children are sons and daughters in the biblical convention. Children are members of a tribe, our descendants. Children are the individual products of particular influences or circumstances.

Therefore, they belong to families, communities and the society at large. For this reason, it is the responsibility of parents, government, community and the society to look after the well-being of these ones, who need to be guided, trained and protected: because they are children. Moreover, it is better and more reasonable to catch them young, rather than waiting until they get to the stage when they want to discover who they are, and to experiment with the good and the bad of the Earth that they inhabit.

I have tried to examine the three discourses of childhood: the Puritan, the Tabula Rasa (blank slate), and Rousseau's Romantic ideas. The Puritan discourse holds that children are inherently evil. Hobbes, an English philosopher (1588-1679) suggested that children, and indeed people, are innately evil. Contrary to the suggestion of Hobbes, another philosopher, Locke (1632-1704) rejected all notions that children are born with any qualities of goodness or evil, but he maintained that children come into the world as a tabula rasa. He further suggested that the child is born with potential, which through the right guidance, and the right sort of experience, could develop into reason. Locke believed that experience shapes the child; that given the right kind of environment and education, the child will become rational, self-controlled and a responsible citizen.

Finally, Rousseau (1712-78), the eighteenth-century French philosopher, dismissed the idea of children being either inherently evil or a tabula rasa. He held that children were born naturally good and innocent and that it is through experience that human beings learn evil. Rousseau believed that a child's heart is pure and angelic in nature but is corrupted by society.

On considering the three discourses of childhood, one can see clearly that the Romantic discourse and the idea of tabula rasa can work hand in hand because it can be likened to what is written in King James' version of the Holy Bible. When the disciples came to Jesus and asked him who is the greatest in the kingdom of heaven, to answer their question he called a little child and set him in the midst of the disciples saying: "Verily I say unto you, except ye be converted, and become as little children, ye shall not enter into the kingdom of heaven. Whosoever therefore shall humble himself as this little child, the same is greatest in the kingdom of heaven."

This goes a long way to explain the innocence of children. Children learn to do wrong things over time. Considering the process of birth and growth, it shows clearly that children are naturally innocent; but adults start taking away the innocence of children, even from conception, by way of speech, action and even the food that is eaten. Pregnant mothers smoke without considering the effects it may have on the unborn child.

When the babies are born they are harmless, helpless, speechless and naked, and this is where tabula rasa comes in; because they have to learn how to sit up, how to crawl, how to walk, how to talk, even how to feed. Children learn from what they see and their environment plays a vital role in their attitude and growth; and it takes courageous, positive and self-controlled parents to train a good and courageous child. It can be imagined, that if the training of a child commences the very day the child was born, he will grow up with wisdom and eventually become a reasonable and productive adult.

Children are like buildings which you continue to construct on a daily basis; if you stop constructing them, they will cease to progress. The construction is supposed to start from the moment they are born; so instead of thinking of how to decorate the baby's room, the type of toys to hang around the cot; the best thing is to start planning how to train that child. Moreover, the best way to pass on wisdom to children is by listening and talking to them. But before that can be done, one has to develop a good and lasting relationship with the children; which also has to be nurtured on a daily basis because even a new born baby, while sucking the mother's breast, is looking straight into the mother's eyes. Mothers that breast-feed their babies can attest to this. That child is passing a message to the mother with his or her eyes and it is the duty of the mother to capture that message and maintain that closeness, even as that child is growing.

A child cannot be trained at a distance. Every second spent with a child is worth more than millions of gifts. Every child loves to be with his parents, especially the mothers, so it is very important for parents to spend time with their children as often as possible. By so doing, a strong bond is being created between that child and the parents.

So much importance is attached to the material needs of the children, but it is equally important to take on board their spiritual, mental and emotional well-being at all times, before they start drifting away from the circle of parents and childhood relationships. It is through harmonious and peaceful discussions with children, that adults will make them realise that life is not full of roses. They need to be told from infancy that life is but a mission; sometimes it can be tough and sometimes it can be soft, but that they have to face the journey of life with optimism.

In the world of today children have everything at their own disposal, even at the very early age. They are being exposed to all forms of fun and frivolities in the matter of dressing, eating habits, socialization and even in speech and behaviour. Television and every other modern day electronic device bring it all to their doorsteps, and whatever they are looking at is going directly into their consciousness. Before the children even get up to the age of twelve these days, their innocence is been taken away. But the most important duty, which is to make the children understand the real meaning of life and how to handle misfortunes, is forgotten or sidelined.

Many years ago, a woman took her two-year-old child to a restaurant for dinner. In the middle of the night, the child started having diarrhoea and vomiting; this happened three times in one year. On another occasion, a similar incident happened in the same neighbourhood; then an elderly woman who lives in the same estate asked two questions: 'Is there no kitchen in their houses? Is it not better for us to cook and feed our children in the comfort of our own homes?'

Well human beings create a lot of problems for themselves, then turn around, and start looking for remedies. Children are being taken through many short cuts, because adults and parents like cutting corners. Yet, if it is calculated properly, you can only discover that the longest way to a destination is through a short cut, while the shortest way to a destination is through a straight-line.

It is very important to let children know that things can go wrong at times, because no matter how wealthy one might be, things can always go wrong. If it is not physical, it can be emotional or mental trouble. In situations like these, adults who are not well equipped with enough emotional and mental strength may tremble and feel suicide is the last resort. Adults have a lot of emotional baggage, which they carry along with them, in the same way as children do. Moreover, the only way for parents to know the emotional state of their children is to keep the relationship between them and their children cordial. However, if it is the opposite, then the parents must use patience, diplomacy and wisdom with their children, so that they can see that they can confide in them; when this happens, it is only then that the parents will discover that children have a wide emotional landscape.

In the process of writing this book, I did some deep emotional and mental searching, trying to fathom out the real nature of children and what it takes to train a good, responsible and optimistic child, with a solid and unwavering mental and emotional status. Then I discovered that it takes the word of God to construct that kind of a child, because I saw where it is written in the *Bible*: "Train up a child in the way he should go: and when he is old, he will not depart from it."

When I read the words of Solomon in the *Book of Proverbs*, where he told his children not to consent when wrongdoers entice them, I just instantly believed that if children are told the same thing these days, they will grow up to lift adults up when they are falling. But I also remembered that one cannot give what he does not have, because adults have to choose the way of wisdom before they can choose it for their children.

When Christmas is drawing near the ultimate concern and desire is what Santa will bring for the children: any adult that meets a child on the way, the first question he is going to ask is 'is Santa coming?' Then, after Christmas, the story will change. The question now becomes, 'Did Santa come? He brought something I am sure?' Yet that particular child has no notion of what Christmas is all about and why it should be celebrated. Children have their minds set on what they are going to get from Santa during Christmas. It does not matter whether there are enough resources to match their expectations with action. It does not matter if the parents have to go borrowing. On the day of Christmas, only a few people may go to church, because on the Christmas Eve many adults might have already drunk themselves to stupor, even in front of the children. Then before the middle of January, everybody is bankrupt. Now the story takes another dimension: 'It is a very difficult year with a very tight budget.' While he or she is talking, they are smoking, yet there is no money: but there is always a reserve for cigarettes and alcohol.

Prudence and extravagance open their doors to anyone who pays for admission. However, most of the time prudence is an orphan, because nobody tries to knock on his front door unless he or she is forced to. By then, though, it might be too late. Extravagance, on the other hand, has too many friends: everybody knocks on its doors and windows, even when there is no want. People force themselves in, simply to satisfy their passing whims, which they soon regret once the novelty is over.

One may feel like asking yesterday to come back today, but unfortunately, it is irreversible. Even at that, if the light of luck shines a little, all the pains of yesterday would be forgotten and once again, people would get carried away with useless and selfish carnal desires that are short lived.

When all hopes are lost, we feel that the best solution is suicide. But is that the end? Suicide is not the answer because no one knows where we are going. If someone takes his or her life, that person has only stopped his or her body from functioning: because the body is just for function. The brain is just for intellect and wisdom. Spirits do not die. There is no consideration as to what happens to the spirit after the body has stopped functioning. However, it should be considered, because there is no probability that suicide will bring someone's problems to an end: the body would be absent from the earth but the spirit would certainly be present somewhere.

Already it is been programmed that everybody is going to die and no matter how long we live, life is very short. It is only our spirit that is connected to our creator. Is it justified for a human being to take his life? I do not know where but I read a place in the Bible where it is written that the hairs of our head are numbered and that none of them shall fall off without the consent of God. This statement is a sure indication that whatever human beings are going through in life, God is already aware.

Again, there is a need for caution: no one knows whether it is right for someone to take his or her life. The rate of suicide in Christendom is shocking. Worst still, it is affecting the children because children learn from what they see and hear. Therefore, it is time for humans to retrace their steps to God, whom we have exchanged for material things. Someone may ask, if God is God and if he is alive, why am I going through hardship? That is a good question, but one should also remember that everything that is happening around us has been programmed to happen even before we were born: although most of the present day predicaments are self-imposed. But looking at the core prayer, our Lord's Prayer, we will discover that it was programmed; that there will be temptation and it comes in diverse ways, but it is only those who endured temptation that will find out the goodness of the world.

Jesus, who taught the prayer to his disciples, knew that there is going to be temptation always. That is why it says in the book of Matthew: "lead us not into temptation, but deliver us from evil", which means it has been programmed that that temptation is going to be there. That was why Jesus begged God to make sure that he would deliver us from evil, since it is destined that temptation will always be there.

The world is like a school and I have never seen or heard of any school that does not have examinations. That is the reason why there are teachers: so that they will prepare the students for the examination day. Again, there is nothing wrong in trying and failing, because it is better for one to try rather than not try at all. When trying, it is also better to try something and fail than to try nothing and succeed.

If one is passing through hard times, the question is, if there is God, why am I going through all this? Does he know that you are going through tough times? Yes he does. Could he have prevented those evil days? Yes, he could have prevented them. Then why didn't he prevent them? He did not prevent them because he wants to create a redemptive value out of them. That redemptive value can only be created if one does not take laws into one's own hands. The world is becoming a terrible place to live in because of man-made liberty and freedom; but liberty without constraint will only produce anarchy, which is being witnessed in the world of today.

There are a lot of festivities here on Earth and children being giving more than they can handle. But directly or indirectly they are being exposed to dangerous delusions: such as the delusion that there is no need to save for the rainy day; that life is all about enjoyment; that they will never lack for anything physically, emotionally or mentally. But if at every given opportunity, whenever we sit down with our children, we connect with them, make use of little holidays to teach them how they can equip themselves with wisdom, integrity and perseverance so that they can withstand the storms of life, whenever it comes, I have no doubt in my mind that those children will be happier.

Technology is good but it is doing a lot of damage to the children as well as adults. More sophisticated technologies are on the way and there is nothing one can do about it. It is not going to get any better, it is going to get darker; but adults should stand upright and fight that battle with positive minds. It is good for children to be treated occasionally. It should be done with caution however, and at the same time supported in some moral and reasonable way: because one of the problems in the world of today is laxity.

The world is changing every day. Technology is advancing but the only thing that remains the same is the word of God. There is nothing ancient or modern in the word of God. Having said that, it does not mean that the word of God is not being diluted. One might ask why are there too many churches in the world of today, especially in Africa. In most countries in Africa, almost every street has a church and almost every family has a pastor because that is where the business is. They are worshiping the god of money, wealth and dubious attitude.

Suicide is not the answer and it must never be. If we learn how to handle misfortunes, how to turn a negative situation into a positive one, we will discover that human beings have dominion over obstacles that may stand in our ways. This is equally true for our children.

The world is like a battlefield: human beings fight against lots of forces that seem to be stronger than they are. Moreover, we cannot subdue those forces through human endeavour. The only way is for humans to put their trust in the Creator, because he has no respect for rank. What status anybody has means nothing to him; his will is that it shall be well with the inhabitants of the earth, regardless of who they are. He cares for everybody and His power is not restricted; His will will be done, and everything depends on the measure through which you follow His will.

When you consider life in the western world and that of the third world (Africa), you will discover that there is a great difference between the two. There is a lot of cultural discrepancy the world over. In some African cultures, mine included, children are advised behind closed doors at a very early age. This is done consistently as that child is growing up. It is done every night. It is called African folklore: the children are spoken to in proverbs and interpretation then follows, then questions. They are also given responsibility at the same time, like the first born child in a family is given the responsibility of looking after the younger ones: not because he or she is not seen as a child but because he or she is older than the others and has to help in looking after them. Because it is believed that if the oldest child is good and positive, and that the rest of the children will follow the same footsteps. This is passed on from generation to generation and the common saying in African families is, 'my son or my daughter, remember the son or daughter of whom you are.' Therefore that child, as he or she is growing up, will always have that in mind, and he takes responsibility to make the younger ones see reasons why they have to be good, industrious and courageous.

In time of misery and hopelessness, it is good to think about many people in this world who are living like birds of the air: they do not know what is going to happen in the next second. They have no access to food, water or shelter. Yet they are living and hoping that things will get better someday.

Recently a friend sent me photos of a famine in Somalia.[1] After looking at them I forgot all my personal worries. It seemed pointless feeling trapped by negative thoughts and self-preoccupation when compared with the predicament that other people find themselves in. Unfortunately, I cannot help these people; I wish that I could but all I could do was lift up my hands and pray for them. Everybody can do the same. So forget everything that you have left behind and keep pressing forward.

Apart from the fact that adults need to construct the life of children, life generally needs consistent construction. As human beings, there is a need to design a pattern of behaviour to help us to construct our lives in reasonable ways, especially in decision-making processes. Taking constructive positive steps in problem solving will help to eliminate self-condemnation and negative thoughts. Thus, Bonham Carter[2] held that constructive behavioural therapy could provide a set of helpful techniques that can assist in identifying and dealing with negative thoughts, in a sensible and practical way of improving the quality of life and making reasonable decisions. Life is full of negatives and positives, but it is only when one allows negativity to predominate over positivity that one tends to make stupid and damaging decisions.

Human thoughts are full of distortion and errors. So learning is very important for life improvement purposes: because one needs to learn new ways that can correct the distorted thinking, which in turn can create a more balanced life. But sometimes we are preoccupied by self-imposed dilemmas that put one in the frontline of the hottest battle, where one finds oneself in the valley of decision. At that point, if you allow the negative to prevail, you might be left no hope of a better tomorrow. Therefore, you are thinking that suicide is the answer, whereas it is not because it creates more problems than the living can contend with. Again, even the dead do not know where the spirit is heading to. Therefore, even when the going is good, one needs to ask always what will happen to the spirit when the body stops functioning.

It is quite unfortunate that the dead cannot speak: otherwise, one could suggest that the dead be asked what happens after death. But I have heard many times, and seen on the television, that some psychics do communicate with the dead. If it were so, one would imagine that it would be very good if they should enquire from the dead and find out what the spirit world is like; whether human beings have the right to take their own lives. Because this mission of survival is not just one person's battle, it is supposed to be collective.

So he who knows how to sing let him sing and turn the sorrows of men to joy.

He who knows how to dance let him dance and appease the spirits of men.

He who knows how to preach the Gospel let him preach and return the hearts of men to the worship of God and the service of mankind.

Where the prophets of the doom are, let them stop prophesying doom and prophesy hope and aspiration to the hearts of men.

He who has, let him share with he who has not.

Physicians should treat the sick and give them hope of a better tomorrow; and let them remember that they treat and God heals.

Those in leadership should lead with passion and consideration, while those that are led should remember to pray for those in leadership, because they are in the frontline of the battle.

Men should rise up to their duties and present themselves as exemplary leaders in their various homes.

It takes two to tango but, according to Solomon, homes are made through the wisdom of women but a foolish woman plunders her home with her own hands with the devil's assistance (*Proverbs* 7:14). Therefore, women should, take a stand, and carry the war to that gate of hell called suicide, so that it will not prevail.

Families bind together, friends team up, communities gather together, societies rise up in the challenge to see children protected and given rights of participation and freedom of speech.

The world is very small and yet very large and full of ups and downs, but is suicide the solution to our problems? Absolutely not. It is not because we have heard of Heaven and Hell; and if we take our life in order to escape from the misfortunes of life, is there any possibility that we are going to Heaven? I do not know. But I do know that life is already very short, no matter how long we live, and death will surely come because it is a natural end to the functioning of the body. But what happens to the spirit after death? I do not know.

What if, after death, the spirit cannot rest in peace, because life was forced out of the body? That is a question everyone has to answer, both young and old.

Is there Heaven? Is there Hell? Who knows: but I would rather believe that there is Hell and Heaven, and die and find out that there is no Hell or Heaven; than to believe that there is no Hell or Heaven and die, only to find out that Heaven is real and Hell is real. Then it will be too late, because I will have lost eternity.

REFERENCES

1. DenverPost.com. *Photos: Somalia Famine*. Posted Aug 03, 2011.
   http://blogs.denverpost.com/captured/2011/08/03/captured-somalia-famine/4538/
2. Bonham Carter, D. 'Cognitive Behavioural Therapy' in Bonham Carter (eds.) *Life Coaching Newsletter*, 2012. www.davidbonham-carter.com

ABOUT THE AUTHOR

Joy C. Agwu is a Nigerian-born author who lives in Ireland. Her writing reflects a pre-occupation with themes of family, faith, community, spirituality, psychological well-being.

For more information about Joy's work, including new and forthcoming titles, please visit her official website at:

www.JoyAgwu.com

ALSO BY JOY C. AGWU

The Echo of a Troubled Soul

A story of family and friendship that also deals with the consequences of grief, pain, sorrow and loss. It is a story of redemption on the journey of recovery.

Following a spate of tragedies Tom is left alone; weighed down by breavement and consumed with grief. His patience and self-control have been stretched to the limit. He goes in search of comfort and companionship and, unfortunately, finds them in alcohol. However this turns out to be the wrong step in the right direction. It is his irrational behaviour during one drunken episode that brings Tom, Larry, Jane and Nora together.

Rescuing Tom from his descent into self-destruction proves to be a fateful decision for Larry, Jane and Nora. Little do they realise at the time, but they each hold the key to unanswered questions in their own lives too.

"Always wear knowledge like a wristwatch: bring it out when you need it because, when you stop learning, you will start dying. Life is too short and it is easier to forgive than to take the path of revenge."

First published in 2013. ISBN 978-0-9571157-6-7
Also available in e-book editions from
Kindle and Smashwords

I Live by the Gun

Edward is a successful family man who has built a happy life around him. Tragedy strikes however, when he is gunned down one day by violent criminals. He leaves behind a widow and two young children, who continue to enjoy the support of Edward's wider

family circle after his death. They are also supported by Edward's close friend, Mr Adams and his family.

Turmoil enters the ranks when Edward's older brother, Robert, citing local traditions, announces his intention to take Edward's place, by moving into the family home of his late brother. Robert's own family, from whom he is estranged, oppose his bid. His father also strongly warns against this course, "Lest tragedy and pestilence befall you." He advises Robert that, "Any tradition that does not add value to our lives has to be thrown away."In *I Live by the Gun*, Joy C. Agwu explores the theme of conflict that arises when traditional hierarchies are confronted by the demands for modernisation. It can be read as an affirmation of human rights and individual autonomy in particular. The burden of 'culture and traditions', when invoked in an anachronistic manner, weigh most heavily on women and children, often serving as a pretext to impose conditions of servitude upon already disadvantaged people.

First published in 2014. ISBN 978-1494453251
Also available in e-book editions from
Kindle and Smashwords

Coming Soon

The Cry Within by Joy C. Agwu. Publication date: 2014. For more information, please visit **www.JoyAgwu.com**, where you can also sign up to receive free e-mail notifications about new and forthcoming titles.

MARK THE GENIUS

by Sandra Agwu

Mark is a very talented and intelligent young student. At school his friends are Lucy, Michael and Tim. All of the other pupils, and even some of the teachers, look to Mark when various problems arise. But being a genius is not always plain sailing: it has its downsides too.

Mark the Genius is a book about school, containing

an important first-hand account of the best days of our lives. It reminds us of a time when dreams, hopes and aspirations are filled with the idea of nothing more than "games for homework, games instead of lessons and a trip to the park for break time?"

Sandra Agwu lives and goes to school in Co. Kerry. She enjoys reading, writing and playing the piano. She is just eight years old but what she has written offers a wealth of experience. Reading it, you will soon see why.

She is currently working on a second instalment of school life adventures. It goes by the working title of *Bob the Bully*.

First published in 2014. ISBN 978-1494453497
Also available in e-book editions from
Kindle and Smashwords
For more information, please visit www.JoyAgwu.com